# THE HIDDEN Vv ʌ ʏ OF LOVE

## Jean-Pierre de Caussade's Spirituality of Abandonment

BARRY CONAWAY

SLG Press
Convent of the Incarnation
Fairacres Oxford OX4 1TB

ISBN 0 7283 0152 0
ISSN 0307-1405

Printed and Bound by Will Print, Oxford, England

*Cover Photograph: The Sea at Bardsey Island*
*© Peter Hope Jones*

'Yes, if one could only leave the hand of God to do its work,
one would reach the most eminent perfection.
All souls would reach it, for it is offered to all.'
*Père de Caussade*

'A teacher must ultimately be judged by the great principles
of his doctrine. But it is not the least merit of Caussade that
he may be read by those to whom theory means little, and
who ask of a book nothing but that it may lead them to God.'
*Dom David Knowles*

'For us let it be enough to know ourselves to be in the place
where God wants us,
and carry on our work, even though it be no more than the
work of an ant,
infinitesimally small, and with unforeseeable results. Now is
the hour of the garden
and the night, the hour of the silent offering: therefore the
hour of hope:
God alone, faceless, unknown, unfelt, yet undeniably God.'
*Abbé Monchanin*

# I

## Caussade's Life and Times

THOMAS MERTON once observed that in the spiritual life we are always beginners—that is, no matter how advanced along the Way we may seem to be, we all need a mentor. And what a blessing it would be to find a wise and godly guide who could help broaden our spiritual horizons to include everything that happens to us, the ordinary and painful as well as the elevated and inspiring, and could teach us how to experience these as a means of extraordinary grace! Over the years many have discovered such a trusty guide in one who quietly insists that 'the most eminent perfection ... is offered to all'. His name, Jean-Pierre de Caussade.

That an obscure eighteenth-century Jesuit who wrote only one rather dry and unsuccessful spiritual textbook, under a pen-name mistakenly attributed to someone else, should now be ranked with St Teresa of Avila and St John of the Cross amongst the greatest spiritual guides is puzzling, to say the least. This, however, is what has happened to Père de Caussade. Henri Bremond calls him 'the incomparable Caussade' but because his one publication went unremarked, Bremond can find no place for him in his great *Literary History of Religious Thought in France*. Caussade's teachings come to us indirectly, from two works which did not see the wider light of day until more than a century after his death. In the first of these, his *Letters and Counsels*, written in the period between 1730 and 1742, from Caussade's mid-fifties to the age of sixty-seven, we get the picture of a man of profound prayer, great spiritual experience and considerable mystical gifts; vivacious, wise and deeply human. Of his writing Fr John Joyce SJ said, 'The style is the man ... tender, sympathetic and humorous. He is subtle but logical, humble but sure, straight, forceful and firm, yet gently persuasive and always encouraging and patient … No wonder his *Treatise and Letters* have become one of the favourites among spiritual classics.'[1]

The *Treatise* to which Fr Joyce refers is Caussade's posthumous masterpiece, compiled from letters and notes of his talks by one of his main correspondents, Mother Thérèse de Rosen. From 1740 the manuscript was circulated privately in various forms. But it was not until 1861 that it was finally arranged by the Jesuit, Paul Ramière, and published under the title *L'Abandon à la Providence Divine* (usually translated as *Self-Abandonment to Divine Providence*). Since then it has been generally acknowledged to be one of the great spiritual classics. It has been called 'a revelation of light and truth';[2] and Dom John Chapman, himself a distinguished spiritual director, wrote, 'I have found no writer so helpful to myself as Fr. Jean-Pierre de Caussade. He speaks from experience and from the heart. His words are lighted up with a magic splendour by his enthusiasm and zeal.' Indeed, Caussade speaks with an integrity and clarity of vision that comes from his great love for and deep union with God. And despite their fragmentary origin, the profound coherence and unity of his thought weave his teachings into a wonderful seamless web.

But before we explore Caussade's thought and its relevance for us today, we need to say something about his life and about the religious climate in which his own spiritual practice and teachings developed.

Caussade lived during the last quarter of the seventeenth century and the first half of the eighteenth, but only the barest facts of his outwardly unremarkable life are known. Born near Toulouse in 1675, Caussade entered the Jesuit noviciate when he was eighteen, was ordained priest in 1704, and made his profession in 1708. For the next six years he taught at the Society's college in Toulouse and was then posted to a variety of places as preacher and missioner. In 1729 he was sent north to

2

Lorraine where, at Nancy, he was associated with the Convent of the Visitation, the religious order founded nearly a hundred and twenty years before by St Francis de Sales and St Jeanne de Chantal. In 1731 he was despatched in disgrace to Albi for letting slip what he describes as some 'indiscreet words'. Two years later, rehabilitated, he was back in Nancy where he gave frequent conferences at the house of the Visitation and undertook the spiritual direction of some of the nuns. It is to these women that we owe most of his surviving work. In 1740 he was moved again; first to Toulouse and then to be rector of two Jesuit colleges in turn at Perpignan and Albi. These were posts he thoroughly disliked. In 1746 he returned to Toulouse as the seminary's spiritual director. He died, blind now, in 1751 at the age of seventy-six, bearing this final affliction with courageous fortitude, as befitting his own great principle of abandonment to the will of God.

Jean-Pierre de Caussade reacted against the rigid and complicated spiritual practices of his times, frequently harking back to the simple faith and trust of 'the patriarchs and prophets who were animated and sanctified before there were so many systems and masters of the spiritual life'. (*AI.1.3.*) The conventional spirituality of Caussade's day is described by Simon Tugwell:

> The brave new church of the Tridentine reformation emerged from the dramas and traumas of the sixteenth century with new anxieties and with new certainties. It was a church of 'law and order', and piety, like everything else, was progressively tidied up into well-marked stages, with disciplined spiritual exercises proper to each stage. Well-trained directors were expected to rule over the souls of those who sought a 'spiritual life'. The natural and supernatural were segregated into a far more rigid apartheid than ever before, and strict immigration procedures controlled admission into the realm of 'supernatural prayer'. Just as, doctrinally, the church had retreated to a bastion of securely demarcated orthodoxy, and felt nervous about venturing

outside it, so too in spirituality people felt confident in certain well-mapped devotional exercises [and] any move outside this safe enclosure was dogged by the fear of illusion.[3]

These were the conditions affecting Caussade and those he counselled. It was against this devotional strait-jacket that movements like Quietism, advocating complete passivity and indifference, even to personal salvation, had reacted. The controversy caused by Mme Guyon and the Quietists had come to a head in the late 1690s with Bossuet's attack on the Archbishop of Cambrai, François Fénelon, for his support of Mme Guyon. Unfortunately, the condemnation of Quietism had the secondary effect of discrediting *all* mysticism, and there were some who saw undesirable quietist tendencies in Caussade's own doctrines. It was in this climate of suspicion that, in 1741, Caussade published his catechetical and ponderously titled *Spiritual Instructions on the Various States of Prayer according to the doctrine of Bossuet, Bishop of Meux.*[4] In it, Caussade repudiates the extreme passivity of the Quietists and enlists the doctrine of the arch-orthodox Bishop of Meux himself to put right some of the damage done to genuine contemplation by the Bishop's own campaign against false mysticism. Caussade stresses the need to 'insist a great deal less on past abuses and rather more on the truths which were formerly abused, and are despised nowadays only on account of these ancient abuses'.[5]

It is to these classic and perennial truths of the spiritual life—the core tradition of Christian devotion—that Caussade appeals in both his *Letters* and *L'Abandon*, supplanting the regimented and cautious spirit of the age with the freedom and simplicity of the Holy Spirit, and reasserting the universal and 'glorious liberty of the children of God'.

4

# II

## *Finding God in All Things*

Caussade's treatise *Abandonment to Divine Providence*—the title provides the phrase most commonly associated with him— begins by recalling an earlier, simpler spiritual tradition that centred on an openness to the secret working of God's grace:

> God continues to speak today as He spoke in former times to our fathers when there were no directors as at present, nor any regular method of direction. Then all spirituality was comprised in fidelity to the designs of God, for there was no regular system of guidance in the spiritual life to explain it in detail, nor so many instructions, precepts and examples as there are now. Doubtless our present difficulties render this necessary but it was not so in the first ages when souls were more simple and straightforward. Then, for those who led a spiritual life, each moment brought some duty to be faithfully accomplished. Their minds, incessantly animated by the impulsion of divine grace, turned imperceptibly to each new duty that presented itself by the permission of God at different hours of the day. (*AI.1.1.*)

From the very start we are brought face to face with Caussade's main concerns: the immediacy of our relationship with God and his dealings with us that require no intermediary to explain and assess them; the danger of trusting devotional methods and techniques and the need for simplicity and directness; the recognition that God deals with us through everything that happens to us and the openness that this calls for in terms of awareness and readiness to react to 'the hidden operations of God'.

Caussade is concerned not with religious experience or spiritual self-fulfilment but with *sanctity*, with the path of

5

perfection, a way of holiness dependent solely on realising the divine purpose in our lives. Rather than being felt and perceived, spiritual realities, Caussade maintains, are always accompanied by profound tranquillity and peace. He deplores any sense of progress in the spiritual life beyond 'a progressive inner simplification'. The secret of spiritual achievement lies not in our own efforts but in God's grace—not in 'being perpetually busy in heaping up meditation upon meditation, prayer upon prayer, reading upon reading' but in 'learning from simple souls the great secret of knowing how, from time to time, to hold yourself back a little in peace and silence, attentive before God.' This he calls 'prayer of the heart', the poorest and most humiliating kind of prayer. Caussade accepts that there is a proper place for regulated piety, but stresses that our fathers in the faith, and our Lady herself, had no 'method' and that their principal director was God himself. As a wise and much sought-after spiritual director, Caussade was certainly not against direction, but he saw the constricting influence of many directors as an obstacle to the movement of the Holy Spirit. (*AI*.1.3.)

Begin at the beginning, look to the ordinary and unexceptional … Caussade's first concern is not that we should succeed in reaching some exalted spiritual goal but that we should find God in all things and know that he gives himself to us in everything; that we should recognize all that happens to us as part of the divine purpose. 'We can find God everywhere without the least effort', he writes, 'because He is truly present to those who seek Him with all their hearts, although they may not always be aware of His presence.' (*LII*.10.) We are fools not to recognize and seize hold of God and see his holiness in all things. He calls us 'dreamers who, though knowing the roads that lead to all the towns, lose their way going to their own house'. (*AI*.2.8.) All too often we are like Jacob; careless about the treasure we possess, we overlook what is right before our eyes: 'Truly, God is in this place and I knew it not'. We must

6

take God's omnipresence seriously and recognize that 'everything proclaims Him, everything gives Him to you. He walks by your side, is around you, and within you.' (*AII.3.5.*)

In spite of suffering and evil, the love of God ever radiates to us, like 'that sublime sun which, from dawn to dusk, however heavy the clouds which hide it, illuminates, warms, and inspires us'. The key to this realization is *faith*. Without faith we cannot see the 'divine Providence which regulates and arranges everything for our greater good, poor ignorant creatures that we are, as blind as moles living underground'. (*LI.3.*) That faith is in a God whose 'divine activity floods the whole universe and pervades every creature; wherever they are it is there; it goes before them, with them, and it follows them; all they have to do is to let the waves bear them on'. (*AI.1.3.*) Everywhere is the theatre of God's loving Providence. Everything is 'God's touch' because 'we live in God, bathed in His action ... our whole environment is God's hand upon us.' All that happens is woven into the tapestry of his over-arching design and purpose. 'There is nothing so small, or so apparently insignificant which God does not ordain or permit, even to the fall of a leaf', says Caussade (*LI.10*). It is we, confined by the veil of our natural vision, who cannot see. 'If we could lift the veil, and if we were attentive and watchful, God would continually reveal Himself to us, and we should see His divine action in everything that happens to us, and rejoice in it. At every occurrence we should say: "It is the Lord", and we should accept every fresh circumstance as a gift of God.' (*AI.2.1.*)

When we find God in everything 'we are rich enough'—we have everything, including the means of our perfection which 'is there all the while in everything that comes to meet you' (*AII.3.5*). It follows that we must trust implicitly in God and his methods which are usually hidden from us by the fog of our self-love and pride. And if we cannot recognize a situation as being sent by God then at least we are to accept it as being part of his will. Thus Caussade can say that nothing distresses him.

He tells us how, when things get bad and he cannot cope, 'I place all my needs in the hands of that good Providence from whom I hope all things. I thank Him without ceasing for all, accepting all from His divine hand.' (LI.5.) 'Things often go perfectly', he says, 'and then I return thanks to God for it, but sometimes everything goes wrong and I bless Him for that equally and offer it to Him as a sacrifice'. (LI.4.)

It is said of the late Fr Christopher Bryant SSJE that he would listen compassionately as those he counselled spoke of their pain, and then he would ask them gently if they had tried *thanking* God for it. In the same way, Caussade advises the nuns to thank God for their trials and ordeals; but if this is impossible, he says, they are to submit with as much grace as they can summon, and pray along the lines: 'Lord, I accept as the blessing of your great mercy all pains which make my self-love suffer and all humiliations which crucify my pride'. It is indeed only our egocentricity that blinds us to God's loving Providence, says Caussade. There is nothing, he believes, that may not be turned to good account if, by the grace of God, we stay faithful and attentive in the circumstances in which we find ourselves. As an example he cites the biblical story of Tobias who dines on the fish that leap out of the Tigris to attack and devour him, and even finds in them the medicine to cure his ailing father!

Caussade tells one of the nuns to imitate Fénelon, 'the holy Archbishop of Cambrai, who said of himself, "I endure all until the worst comes to the worst and then, finally, I find peace in complete self-abandonment"'. (LI.1.) It is to the meaning of that abandon that we now turn.

# III

## *Let Go, Let God*

Caussade's principal teachers were St Francis de Sales (1567-1622) and St John of the Cross (1542-91). His own thought combined the warmth and humanity of the first with the intensity and depth of the second; but as a Jesuit he inherited from his spiritual father, St Ignatius Loyola, not only the ability of 'finding God in all things' but also the predominating belief that the proper purpose of all things is to be a pliable and ready instrument in the hands of God. The overall aim of Ignatius' *Spiritual Exercises* is to help the retreatant to order his life according to the will of God, a purpose summed up in Ignatius' *Suscipe*: 'Take, Lord, all my liberty, receive my memory, my understanding and my whole will. Whatever I have and possess Thou hast given me; to Thee I utterly surrender it for Thy direction. Give me the love of Thee only with Thy grace and I am rich enough; nor ask I anything beside.'

Again and again, Caussade repeats the substance of this prayer in every variation. The sacrificing of oneself to God, he says, is the 'great and solid foundation of the spiritual life', 'becoming so completely forgetful of self as to regard oneself as a chattel, sold and delivered, to which one no longer has any right'. (*AII.2.1.*) Caussade proclaims his message of *self-abandonment* to the will of God with ecstatic delight: 'I should like to cry out everywhere, "Abandonment! abandonment!" and again "Abandonment!" unbounded and unreserved' (*LI.8*), for only 'in proportion to our abandonment and confidence in God will our lives be holy and tranquil'. (*LI.3.*) Francis de Sales had spoken of our education in 'the school of Calvary' and Caussade insists that the secret of all spiritual growth lies in self-giving and self-forgetting: one must 'give oneself to God and

9

afterwards forget oneself completely', he says, practising a trusting and childlike surrender to the guidance of the Holy Spirit, and submitting to God's will in every situation and circumstance.

We are to do this not by anxiously searching to discover what God actually wills for us (which was what the formal and inflexible spirituality of Caussade's contemporaries sought to do), nor by conscious acts of resignation and deliberate indifference (which was the Quietist solution), but by simply receiving what comes to us, moment by moment, and abandoning ourselves to that: accepting and willing everything because it comes as God's will for us here and now, in this particular instant. Caussade gives a personal example of this process from his uncongenial posting to Perpignan:

> I left the mother-house, which I loved, with a peace and liberty of spirit which astonished even myself. More still! When I arrived at Perpignan I found a large amount of business to attend to, none of which I understood; and many people to see and deal with; the Bishop, the steward, the king's lieutenant, the Parliament, the garrison staff. You know what horror I have always entertained for visits of any sort, and above all for those of grand people. Well! none of these have given me any alarm; in God I hope to find a remedy for everything, and I feel a confidence in divine Providence which enables me to surmount all difficulties. Besides this I enjoy peace and tranquillity in the midst of a thousand cares and anxieties, such as I should have imagined ought naturally to overwhelm me. (*LII.3.*)

The teaching is supremely demonstrated though, says Caussade, in the mystery of the Annunciation to the Blessed Virgin Mary. Our Lady's 'Be it unto me according to thy word'—her 'Yes' to God—has in it, he says, 'all the mystical theology of our ancestors'.

Francis de Sales had compared the committed heart to a ball of wax in the hands of God, 'a heart without choice of its own, equally disposed for all things, with no other aim than to do

10

God's will'. In the same vein, Caussade likens our self-abandonment to a statue in the making, passive in the hands of the Master Sculptor, chiselled and shaped by the Master's will to attain his purpose—'the completion and perfection of the work'. In another instance, he speaks of a servant fixing his gaze on his Master in order to perceive and promptly do his bidding. And again, compiling a whole catalogue of analogies, he explains that self-abandonment requires us to be as light as a feather, liquid as water, simple as a child, reacting to every moment of grace like a floating balloon; like molten metal filling whatever shape God decides to pour us into; or like an artist's canvas, waiting only for what God paints upon us. (AII.2.6.)

Trusting in this way to God's grace and the guidance of the Holy Spirit means for the most part that we have to 'work in the dark'. Caussade likens 'the soul that has abandoned itself to God and has eyes only for Him and for its duty' to a tapestry being woven stitch by stitch from the 'wrong' side. The person working on it sees only the stitch she is making, and only when the right side is turned outwards can the full design and beauty of the tapestry be seen. Just as none of this perfection was at all visible while the work was in progress so the soul in its abandonment is transformed by the hidden workings of God's grace. (AII.3.5.) To illustrate this secret transformation that the quiet surrender of abandonment affords, Caussade borrows St Teresa's image of the silkworm, whose remarkable, unseen metamorphoses are like a series of secret deaths and resurrections. Hidden in its cocoon, to all appearances dead, it goes on living and spinning its silk until 'the warmth of grace' hatches it out. (*ibid.*)

Though our stance is to be attentive and passive to the will of God, our response might very well be to a call to activity. It would be wrong, therefore, to interpret Caussade's *abandon* to the will of God as a form of vegetative resignation; it is rather a uniting of our will with God's. 'I do not say that we are to do nothing', he explains. 'To wait with folded arms for everything

11

to drop from heaven would be an absurd and sinful quietism. Therefore while co-operating with God and leaning on Him, we must never leave off working ourselves.' (*LI.5*.) The abandoned soul responds to the will of God in whatever fashion is appropriate to that will; so, says Caussade, 'It is vain to picture any kind of abandonment from which all personal activity is excluded. When God requires action, holiness is to be found in activity.' (*AI.1.8*.) It is a case of 'acting when it is the moment for action, keeping quiet when you should do so, enduring loss when you ought to'. (*AII.3.5*.)

We speak of someone *abandoning* themselves to an emotion or sentiment, or of a swimmer abandoning himself to the waves and current; and by this we mean a kind of letting go, a relinquishing of our control. But the analogy of the swimmer brings out the *dynamic* aspect of abandonment, for although the swimmer lets go and trusts the water to support him, he has to be *active* as well, and be constantly adapting himself to the movement of the sea. This activity has its parallel in the spiritual life where our acts of faith, hope and love are made in response to God's activity in and upon us. Passivity and activity, then, come together: we do whatever needs to be done in a spirit of receptivity; so, says Caussade, we are 'passively active or actively passive'. The important thing is not *what* we are doing or enduring at any particular moment but that *what we are doing or enduring is the will of God for us at that time*. As God's will for us in each new circumstance reveals some new duty, what was best for the moment that has passed may well not be so now. Sometimes there may be nothing for us to do, in which case we should do nothing. At another time God may lead us to a state of total emptiness, and then we must be content with being empty. When we do what is called for as faithfully as we can or suffer it as patiently and as lovingly as possible then, in the eyes of God, what we do is equal to the saintliest of actions. (*AI.1.5*.) Sanctity, says Caussade, lies in this single practice: 'fidelity to the duties appointed by God'. (*AI.1.3*.)

Like all analogies, Caussade's examples of things being shaped or filled and so on must not be pushed too far; they are only partial aids to our understanding of self-abandonment. For those who, like most of Caussade's correspondents, are already well on the road to spiritual maturity, they are useful models, and might help to counteract the impulse to be over-active and too impatient to wait on God. They are clearly applicable to situations which seem to be beyond our power to change, those circumstances which call for patience, endurance and a humble bearing of one's cross. But examples of stone to be carved or swimmers in the sea are less helpful where duty calls us to undertake some uncongenial task—to write a letter when we would rather read the paper, to attend a meeting when we would rather be at home, to go to work when we would rather stay in bed, to visit the sick when we would rather be alone, to say the Office when we are distracted or 'dry'. Many of the things that make up everyday life, though very much part of God's purpose, call for a positive act of will to get them done. For abandonment in these instances we need to look at another, closely connected feature of Caussade's teaching: 'the sacrament of the present moment'.

# IV

## The Sacrament of the Present Moment

Because the universe is flooded with divine activity, every moment is charged with the presence of God and each moment has its part to play in the pattern of his purpose. No moment is without value, for at every instant, says Caussade, God presents himself to us under the guise of some joy or sorrow, some task or duty to be performed. Whatever it contains—pleasure or pain, health or sickness—every moment is potentially 'a stone towards the building of the heavenly Jerusalem' and our means of 'union with God on earth'. (AI.2.1.)

'The present moment', he says, 'is the ambassador who declares God's will. Everything is a help to the soul and is, without exception, an instrument of sanctity. The one thing necessary can always be found for it in the present moment'. (AI.2.10.) God speaks 'to all men by what happens to them from moment to moment' (AI.2.4.) and rather than look, as we might have expected, for the means of holiness in the most exalted places, Caussade teaches that we can find all we need for perfection in the simplest and most immediate circumstances of our lives. Jung told of a student who went to a rabbi and said, 'In the old days there were men who saw the face of God. Why don't we see him any more?' The rabbi replied, 'Because no one nowadays can stoop so low.' The less there is to see, says Caussade, the more there is to believe: in other words, to find God in the tiniest and most ordinary events as well as in the greatest is to have not an ordinary but a great and extraordinary faith. (AI.2.2.)

What God requires is most clearly shown in our ordinary duties and obligations and, however onerous and unappealing these may be, as the messengers of God's will they should be carried out promptly and faithfully with wholehearted commitment. These demands are clear and in them we can see what is needed. But, more often than not, God directs us to some unplanned task or unexpected situation; and then our duty will be to respond to God's new promptings. You feel some impulse to speak or to do something, says Caussade. 'Well, obey this impulse according to the inspiration of grace without stopping to reflect, to reason, or to make efforts. Give yourself up to these things for as long as God wishes without doing so through any self-will.' (*AII.2.6.*)

This last adjuration is clearly important if Caussade's advice is not to be seen as a licence for every whim and self-indulgence. Our response to the inspiration of the present moment is to be disciplined and detached and purged of self-will. To follow this method, 'by which one subsists in God alone, and in the present duty', writes Caussade, 'it is necessary to be detached from all that one feels, and from all that one does. One must restrict oneself to the present duty without thinking of the preceding one, or of the one which is to follow.' (*ibid.*) Like all the great directors, Caussade is anxious to release those who are growing in the life of the spirit to follow the leading of God. But he is addressing those who 'desire to belong to God entirely' and are wholly devoted 'to acquiring the spirit of prayer and the interior life' (*LI.1.*); and the subtle discernment demanded by the present moment indicates that he assumes a certain spiritual maturity and some training in ascetic discipline. Nevertheless, Caussade makes it quite clear that:

> The divine will, working in the soul of a simple ignorant girl by means of sufferings and actions of a very ordinary nature, produces in the depths of her heart a mysterious fulfilment of supernatural life. While a proud man who studies spiritual books merely out of curiosity and without regard for the will of God, receives only the dead letter into his mind, and his heart becomes ever harder and more withered. (*AI.1.5.*)

Nothing in Scripture suggests that the life of the Blessed Virgin was outwardly anything but unremarkable. Her exterior life is very ordinary and simple. She does and suffers the same things as other people in her state of life do and suffer, but

> what treasures of grace lie concealed in these moments filled, apparently, by the most ordinary events. That which is visible might happen to anyone, but the invisible, discerned by faith, is no less than God himself performing great things. O Bread of Angels! heavenly manna! pearl of the Gospel! Sacrament of the present moment! (*AI*.1.2.)

God reveals himself to the humble in the humblest things, says Caussade, while the proud who never see beneath the surface, fail to find him even in great ones.

Just as we read God's word in holy Scripture with the 'eyes of faith', so must we read his word in his actions with a spirit that is 'simple, gentle, yielding, and submissive to the faintest breath of scarcely perceptible impressions'. (*AII*.2.6.) 'In the state of abandonment', he says, 'the only rule is the duty of the present moment. In this the soul remains lovingly passive in God's hands, receiving and following all the inspirations of grace.' (*AII*.2.6.) This is the grain of mustard seed, the 'treasure that none discover because they suppose it to be too far away to be sought'. But its location is no secret; on the contrary,

> The treasure is everywhere, it is offered to us at all times and wherever we may be. All creatures pour it out with prodigality, and it flows like a fountain through every faculty of body and soul, even to the very centre of our hearts. If we open our mouths they will be filled. (*AI*.1.3.)

Christ seeks to unite himself to us. For this reason, says Caussade, 'every moment of our lives is a sort of communion with divine love, continuously producing in our souls the fruits of that communion in which we receive the body and blood of God.' All that happens to us is like a 'mystery and sacrament of love' comparable to 'the most august mystery of all.' Our sufferings, our actions, 'all spiritual impulses that are in the divine design' are the sacramental species under which God gives himself to us. To receive each present moment as a sacrament assumes the exercise of what Caussade calls 'the sole rule of saints'—the discipline of ordinary things which abandonment imposes. In turn, that asceticism must be complemented by prayer, a personal relation with the mystery of God and the channel of his love and grace.

# V

## *Prayer and the Present Moment*

Self-abandonment to divine Providence means quite simply the abandonment of *self*, 'total self-renunciation for the sake of living the life of grace according to the divine operation'. (*AI*.1.1.) However, as *The Imitation of Christ* points out, it is 'only with difficulty that a man is stripped of self-love'. (Book II, ch.ix.2.) How, then, are we to die to self and become alive in Christ? We are, says Caussade, to do it both through the ascetic challenge of the present moment and through prayer. Sacrifice and prayer support and require each other. The former, through a perpetual surrender to God, is a way that is no less mortifying than the discipline of the desert—the place of trial and purgation, of solitude and detachment—where, stripped of self and all distractions and evasions, the soul is opened to God. Thus Caussade describes self-abandonment as 'a desert in which the simple soul sees nothing but God alone'. (*AII*.2.4.) And on one occasion he confesses to being 'in a veritable desert, alone with God', a state where 'exterior solitude is combined with a great interior emptiness'. (*LI*.6.)

Prayer, too, for Caussade takes on the ascetic simplicity of the desert, and his teaching here is reminiscent of the Desert Fathers' emphasis on 'purity of heart'. The following observation by Thomas Merton is totally in keeping with the teaching of Père de Caussade:

> The Desert Fathers did not imagine themselves ... to be mystics, though in fact they often were. They were careful not to go looking for extraordinary experiences, and contented themselves with the struggle ... to keep their minds and hearts empty of care and concern, so that they might altogether forget themselves and apply themselves entirely to the love and service of God.[6]

18

Caussade stresses that there is no magic formula. The road can be long and great patience and humility are needed, for we have to be 'purged and purified and refined' of all the imperfections and barriers that hinder God's free access to us. He quotes St Francis de Sales' dictum that perfection cannot be 'put on like a dress'; nor does it consist in many acts and techniques, he says. On the contrary, 'the further we advance, the more it pleases God to invite us to remain before him in silence and humble recollection'. And in all conditions and circumstances to say constantly from the bottom of your heart, 'My God you wish this, I wish it also. I refuse nothing from your fatherly hand; I accept all, I submit to everything.' In this we echo our Lord's own 'Thy will be done', says Caussade. Indeed, he believed that this 'matchless prayer given to us by Jesus Christ' and recited not only with the lips but 'constantly in the depths of the heart' encapsulates the whole meaning of self-abandonment.

The more one can keep oneself in 'holy interior simplicity' with 'peace in the depth of the heart and centre of the soul', says Caussade, 'the more will God himself make you advance'. (LII.20.) He invites us to consider what happens to green wood in the fire. Before it can burn it will hiss and writhe until it has been dried enough for the flames to take hold of it. In the same way the fire of divine love acts upon us to purify, refine and clear away our 'evil inclinations of self-love'. Only then can we catch fire and burn with that same divine flame of love. (LIV.1.) Through this process of purgation, Caussade says, God begins to live in the soul so that 'it has nothing more of its own, nothing but what He gives it'. (AII.1.1.) If once the soul was cluttered and full, it is now like an empty building that God can occupy. It is becoming increasingly passive under the divine influence. Caussade compares it to 'a child whom one leads where one wishes'. Prayer becomes increasingly simple, animated less and less by our own activity and more and more by the grace of God. We must wait in peace and without anxiety, holding ourselves in 'an attitude of humble docility, calmly and simply keeping our interior gaze fixed on God and our own nothingness'. Given this opportunity, God's grace will 'effect great things in the soul without us knowing what is happening or how He works'. (LII.14.)

But beware: the very desire to excel in virtue and 'succeed' in prayer is a deadly trap—a temptation with which Caussade himself is familiar. He writes:

> I experience impetuous desires of acquiring the gift of prayer, humility, gentleness, the love of God; to this I reply: Let us not think so much about our own interests; my duty is to occupy myself simply and quietly with God, to accomplish his will in all that he asks of me at the moment. That is my task; everything else I leave in the care of God. (LII.1.)

Contrary to all natural assumptions, our own wretched condition, realistically understood and confronted, he says, is worth more to us than any angelic virtue whose merit we attribute to ourselves. (LII.13.) He tells one of the nuns that the 'depths of wretchedness and corruption' into which she has sunk is 'a supreme grace', for it is the foundation of all self-distrust and of utter trust in God. (LIII.1.)

We are to strive for detachment and a mastery of all in ourselves that would pull us apart. The life of prayer is 'a continual struggle against the senses'; and the 'most perfect prayer', Caussade insists, 'is the simplest, and the simplest is the prayer into which less of our own enters, fewer ideas, less imagination or reasoning—the prayer that is formed of a single sentiment long drawn out'. (LII.8.) Prayer must be 'a constant turning of your heart to God or gazing interiorly upon his divine presence'. (LIII.3); by keeping oneself in 'a profound silence' opportunity is given 'for the inmost operations of the Holy Spirit'. We are to pray by 'a simple but actual inclination of the heart, which contains all and says all to God without express words' (LII.21); and to listen 'attentively to the words uttered in the depths of the heart at every moment'. (AI.2.6.) Caussade lists the various names given to this way of prayer: it is called the prayer of loving attention to God; the prayer of a simple looking at God; the prayer of pure faith and simplicity which stretches out to God; the prayer of loving recollection in God; the prayer of self-surrender and self-abandonment to God, which is born of the love of God and always causes a still greater love of God to be born in the soul. (*LII*.21.)

This prayer of simplicity or recollection—'simple interior waiting, silent, peaceful and entirely resigned'—is 'the interior life's first need,' he says. (*LIII*.7.) St. Teresa interprets it as a stage on the way to the prayer of quiet, union and ecstasy. For Caussade, however, it plays a central role; and, because of all that he believes about the promptings of the present moment, he avoids placing it in any schema or setting down hard and fast divisions for the interior life. The prayer of recollection, he tells one of his correspondents, 'is a prayer wholly of love: the heart, reposing sweetly in God, loves him without distinguishing clearly the object of its love, or how this love is produced in it'. (*LII*.10.) And if this prayer should become dry and without sweetness then this too is a blessing, for such a state, he says, may be a far more effective means of sanctity than any which is full of deceptive consolation. Hence he can write to one who has been experiencing difficulty in prayer:

> Do not be anxious for you are far from wasting time in prayer. Doubtless you could pray more tranquilly, and will do so when it pleases God. Yet your prayer will never be more availing or of more worth: for the prayer of suffering and of self-obliteration is the hardest of all and purifies the soul proportionately, causing it to die the sooner to self and to live thereafter only in God and for God. I rejoice in those prayers in which you stand before God like a beast of the field, lost to everything and bowed down by the burdens of every kind of temptation. (*LIV*.1.)

Through such experiences of desolation and apparent failure in prayer the soul is turned from the captivity of discursive reason and the cultivation of self, and exposed to the divine will and

21

action. One enters a state of 'spiritual childhood' (*LII*.3) which is the perfect condition of *abandon*. Above all things, Caussade tells us, 'we must place our reliance upon God, depending upon him for all our wants, putting all our hope in him, running to him in all things', as a child runs to its mother (*LIV*.15). In this vulnerable state even 'our trivial defeats are permitted in order to aid us in practising humility and patience'. From this point of view, such defeats are 'immensely more useful to us than victories spoilt by vain complacency'. (*LVI*.17.) Even the greatest temptations are graces, for they provide 'an interior martyrdom', the field of 'those great struggles and great victories which have made great saints'. (*LV*.443.) Our guide in prayer, says Caussade, should always be simplicity, 'for God loves to see us like children before him' (*LIV*.7.) and the pure in heart are blessed by seeing God.

# VI

## Faith, Love, and Union with God

In his book *Is There Anyone There?* Richard MacKenna tells the story of a walker who is suddenly blown off the clifftop. Luckily, as he falls he manages to cling on to a tree growing from the rock face. He calls for help and after a few agonising moments a voice asks him what he wants. 'Just help me! Save me!' cries the man. 'Very well', the voice replies, 'but if I am to save you, you'll have to trust me'. The anguished man agrees without hesitation. 'This is God speaking', says the voice. 'All you have to do is let go and fall and I will save you.' There is a long pause and then comes a pitiful little cry, 'Is there anybody else there?'[7]

Caussade would bring us to the same brink of commitment. Divine action sets us on unfamiliar paths which we 'follow by divine impulse', he says, and asks: What can one do 'when one is conducted through an unknown country at night across fields where there are no tracks, by a guide who follows his own ideas without revealing his plans ... but abandon oneself to his care?' (*AII.2.7.*) He likens the will of God at each moment to 'an immense, inexhaustible ocean that no human heart can fathom'. Against all our fears and natural resistance we are to plunge into 'the unfathomable depths of this abyss' which challenges our complacent security and threatens to destroy all our illusions and self-delusion, along with 'the idols of sense' and all that keeps us from God. A modern contemplative urges the same chastening course when he writes: 'We should let ourselves be brought naked and defenceless into the centre of that dread where we stand alone before God in our nothingness ... completely dependent upon his providential care, in dire need of the gift of his grace, his mercy, and the light of faith.'[8] The

23

leap of faith into 'the deep abyss of God's love' is death to the old unregenerate self; but, 'if you plunge into this abyss', Caussade assures us, 'you will find it infinitely more vast than your desires'. (AI.2.2.) From the darkness comes light. From death, life. From the abyss of seeming nothingness there comes the mysterious gift of the Spirit to make all things new. Our dependence on this dreadful depth of God is expressed by Pascal in his *Pensées* when he writes that there is in everyone 'the infinite abyss that can only be filled by an infinite and immutable object, that is to say, only by God himself'. (Sect.VII.425.)

Reason and good sense would hold us back, but they must be curbed; our understanding, which 'seeks first place among the divine methods', must be relegated to the last. In our surrender, the 'darkness itself is a light for our guidance; and doubts are our best assurance' (AII.4.1). 'God himself is night to the soul in this life', said St John of the Cross. (*Ascent of Mount Carmel* I.2.) Those who live in a 'state of perfect self-abandonment' and whose lives are motivated solely by the will of God are bound to find the present moment a place of darkness, Caussade tells us, for 'when God lives in the soul, it has nothing left of self but that which He gives it' and the soul is condemned to 'obscurity, forgetfulness, death and nothingness'. (AII.1.1.) While 'the spirit flies to the light, the heart is content with darkness', for when you are in this darkness, as the fourteenth-century mystic Walter Hilton says, 'you are much nearer to Jerusalem than when you are living in the false light [of the senses]'.[9] In this dark night we cannot understand God's action, nor hear his voice; our feelings are dead. Naked faith alone, says Caussade, can then see us through, enabling us to 'pass through and beyond the veils, shadows and, as it were, deaths' that conspire 'to hide the will of God'. (AI.2.2.) Like an X-ray or laser beam (to use a modern image), there

> is nothing that faith does not penetrate and overcome. It passes through the thick darkness and, no matter what clouds

gather, it goes straight to the truth, and holding it firmly will never let it go. (*AI.2.2.*)

Faith is 'the interpreter of God' and leads us to him through 'all that disguises, disfigures and seeks to abolish Him'. We fear to cross this 'obscure region', but Caussade assures us that 'this is precisely your path and the way God wishes you to go. Nothing is surer and more infallible than the darkness of faith. The darker it grows, the more numerous the chasms, the snares, the obstacles that line our path, the greater shall our faith and confidence be.' (*AII.4.1.*)

Pure faith is always accompanied by the fire of divine love, says Caussade; for 'perfection consists in pure love and the exercise of pure love consists in self-abandonment' that 'forms Jesus Christ in the depths of our hearts'. He sees abandonment as a unity of faith, hope and love, and traces all three virtues to the same origin:

> The touch of the Holy Spirit in souls inflamed with His love, is called pure love; but in souls that are plunged in bitterness it is called pure faith because the darkness and obscurity of night are without alleviation. Pure love sees, feels and believes. Pure faith believes without either seeing or feeling. (*AII.1.3.*)

By the illumination of these virtues 'the heart is raised, entranced and becomes conversant with heavenly things' (*AI.2.1*); it sees, like Moses, 'the fire of divine charity burning in the midst of the thorns and is enabled to discover the marvels of heavenly wisdom'. (*AII.2.1.*) To live an unbroken life of faith, says Caussade, would be to enjoy constant contact with the divine—speaking to God as Moses did, face to face. But just as Moses was unable to look upon the full vision of God and had to hide from God's face in the cleft of a rock, so too, says Caussade, in 'the passive state of pure faith' which accompanies abandonment, 'all that God communicates partakes of the nature of that inaccessible darkness that surrounds His throne'. (*AII.4.1.*) But when he transports a soul into that inaccessible darkness, it becomes luminous and the soul is granted 'learned ignorance' to see all while seeing nothing, to hear all while hearing nothing, know all while knowing nothing. Caussade describes it as 'an operation of grace' which we should accept with joy and 'plunge into it and lose ourselves in it for as long as it pleases God'. (*LI*.16.)

This dying to everything that is centred upon our selves, even to spiritual matters, is the hardest thing of all for our reluctant souls to suffer; it is 'a sort of annihilation through which I must pass', writes Caussade, 'in order to rise again with Jesus Christ to a new life, a life all in God'. (*LI*.6.) Union with God cannot be realised without going through this painful transformation. 'Poverty and nakedness of spirit is the last stage to perfect union. It is a true death to self, a most secret, torturing and hardly endurable death; yet a death soon rewarded with a resurrection'. (*LVI*.7.) God teaches the soul by 'pains and contradictions, not by ideas', Caussade tells us. It is only by constant crosses and 'through a long series of mortifications, trials and strippings that one can be established in the state of pure love'. (*AII*.2.2.) Such love 'wears the mask of nothingness'[10] because 'God takes everything from us but innocence, so that we may possess nothing but ourselves alone'. (*AII*.3.2.) It is a total 'self-noughting'. And, most devastating and cruel of all, the 'soul that desires nothing else but the will of God' is now deprived even of the consolation of loving him. 'Perfection is given to it contrary to all preconceived ideas, to all light, to all feeling, by all the crosses sent by Providence, by the action of present duties.' Everything seems far removed from 'the dazzling sublimity of sanctity and all that is unusual in virtue'. (*AII*.3.4.)

Divine union is reached by way of paradox and contradiction, 'by means of things which appear opposed to the end proposed'. (*AII*.4.4.) 'God and His grace', says Caussade, 'are given in a hidden and strange manner'. (*AII*.3.4.) The self is stripped of its last vestiges of spiritual reward and every consoling image of itself. God disappears from sight; and now, instead of leading the soul forward, he seems to be propelling it from behind, 'being no longer its clearly conceived object but its invisible principle'. Only beyond this darkness and desolation does the dawn of illumination break into final union. In the depths of self-abandonment, 'where the soul was to find pure nothingness, it finds the infinite'. (*LI.8.*) Now, in Isaiah's words, 'The wilderness and the desolate places shall be glad, the desert shall rejoice and blossom, and they shall see the glory of the Lord, the majesty of our God.' (Isaiah 35:1-2.) The light shines now in the darkness, the desert blooms. 'By the purity of its secret effects, that very grace that it cannot perceive, gives the soul the hundredfold of what it has taken away'. (*AII.3.4.*) The very deprivation that we suffer is the hidden means of love. Caussade explains that, 'With God, the more one seems to lose the more one gains. The more He strikes off of what is natural, the more He gives of what is supernatural. He is loved at first for His gifts, but when these are no longer perceptible He is at last loved for Himself.' (*AII.4.3.*) Thus does God prepare us by 'apparent withdrawal' for 'that great gift which is the most precious and the most extensive of all, since it embraces all the rest'. (*ibid.*)

> Let us go, then, let us run and fly to that ocean of love by which we are attracted! What are we waiting for? Let us start at once, let us lose ourselves in God, even in His heart, to become inebriated with the wine of His charity. Let us begin at once our journey to Heaven, where the Spouse reveals the secrets of His love to faithful souls. O divine incommunicable secrets that no mortal tongue can describe! Love flows on every side, into those hearts open to receive this divine outpouring. O divine harvest for eternity! it is not possible to praise you sufficiently. And why speak so much about you? How much better to possess you in silence than to praise you with mere words. (*AII.1.8.*)

What are we waiting for? Let us start at once ...

# VII

## Perfection for All

We must always bear in mind that in his own lifetime Père de Caussade's counsel was restricted to the cloister and offered only to those who were set upon a disciplined life of prayer. Rather than presenting any kind of universal primer for the interior life, therefore, his writings take much for granted concerning the spiritual life and leave many things unsaid. Certainly, his teaching was not originally intended for people living 'in the world'; but just as St. Ignatius had made the *Exercises* versatile enough to lead as many souls as possible to a full Christian life, so Caussade, because he believed that 'people in the world as well as souls specially privileged by Providence: kings and their ministers, princes of the Church and of the world, priests, soldiers, tradesmen and labourers, in a word all men', could go far in the life of faith, saw himself as 'a missionary of God's holy will to teach everyone that there is nothing so easy, so ordinary and so ready to everyone's hand as holiness!'. (*AI* 1.9.)

Alongside Caussade's own deep sanctity there runs an equally deep humanity, and whatever he teaches about perfection and the rigours of its attainment, he never loses sight of our inescapable *human* condition. Bernard Bro once remarked that St Thérèse of Lisieux had 'democratized holiness'.[11] Jean-Pierre de Caussade, in fact, had done so a hundred and fifty years before. Everyone can attain sanctity, he insists, 'by the simple use of the means that God, the sovereign director of souls, gives them to do or to suffer at each moment'. (*AI.1.3.*) Both self-abandonment and perfection, through the grace of baptism, are available to all who will 'submit with faith and love to the designs of Providence in everything that is

28

constantly being presented to them to do and to endure, without searching for anything themselves'. This is nothing new, he says, but the oldest way of all, for it is 'the spirituality which sanctified the patriarchs and prophets, the spirituality of all ages and states of life'. (*ibid.*) Its secret lies simply in 'fulfilling with love our lowly and common duties' (*AII.4.3.*), so it can be practised in each and every situation of one's life.

But it is not the easy option, for it directs us on a Christlike path of painful self-donation and Caussade never underplays the sacrifice involved, the seed dying in order to live and bear fruit—though that process too, he insists, is a blessing. Nor is abandonment an inferior alternative to some more exalted spiritual way, for it is the full life of faith that we share with Christ and the saints. Although Caussade wanted 'to make everyone see that they can aim at eminent sanctity', he knew that few of us are faithful enough to attain the more exalted spiritual graces. But though we may fail so often in the necessary faith, the spiritual attainment described and enjoined by Caussade through abandonment and the sacrament of the present moment, remains genuine perfection, not a means to an end but the end itself—true mystical union.

Caussade then is for all those who truly seek God, a steady friend, as David Knowles describes him, to whom both in times of difficulty and in the day to day course of life we can always turn. There is a depth and sureness to his teaching, and to read him is to experience the intimate company of a great spiritual guide upon the journey of faith. In all his words there is a simplicity that hides the profoundest thought; and there is in his counsel a humility and compassion which clothes the sublimest doctrine of perfection with gentleness. Caussade's teaching is for all, and when the time is right no one who would climb the mountain of the Lord can afford to travel without it.

## VIII

*Père de Caussade and the 'Little Flower': A Postscript*

If Caussade looks back to St John of the Cross and St Francis de Sales then he looks forward, too, to St Thérèse of Lisieux (1873-1897). Though they lived more than a hundred years apart, there are some remarkable affinities in the thought and spiritual practice of Caussade and the 'Little Flower'. David Knowles describes it as 'a real and pervading similarity of soul'. Hers was a life wholly dedicated to the will of God, her only ambition to give everything to him. 'I ignored myself and sought myself in nothing', she confessed towards the end of her short life. In John of the Cross, Caussade and Thérèse shared a common ancestry. As a child of Carmel, Thérèse was of direct descent and lived out John's teaching with heroic dedication. She speaks of the annihilating darkness that purifies as a gift of grace, of *le nuit du néant*—'the night of nothingness'—and of the Christ-light that she carried within her, unfelt, unrealized, in total despairing darkness. Like Caussade she was dedicated to a spirituality of abandonment: 'Abandonment is my only guide', she claimed. Like him she saw 'extraordinary ways' of holiness as potential sources of illusion, and rejoices in the very ordinariness of the blessed Virgin's life: 'No rapture, no miracles, no ecstasies embellish your life, O Queen of the Elect'.[12]

It is most unlikely that Thérèse ever read Caussade or even knew of him; yet her autobiography, *The Story of a Soul*, frequently reminds us of her fellow countryman, and her 'little way' is the pure embodiment of self-abandonment. Thérèse's description of it might well be Caussade himself speaking:

> It is the way of spiritual childhood, the way of confidence and abandonment to God. It means that we acknowledge our nothingness; that we expect everything from the good Lord, as a child expects everything from its father. It also means not

30

to believe we are capable of anything, but to acknowledge that it is the good Lord who has placed that treasure in the hand of his little child. Finally, it means that we must not be discouraged by our faults, for children fall frequently. (*Novissima Verba.*)

In one of his prayers (see p. 32 below) Caussade refers to 'holy humiliations which crucify my pride'; and in the following words could almost be speaking of Thérèse:

Souls called by God to a life of perfect abandonment resemble in this respect our Lord, His holy Mother, and St Joseph. The will of God was, to them, the fulness of life. Submitting entirely to this will, they were always in complete dependence on what we might call the purely providential will of God. From this it follows that their lives, although extraordinary in perfection, showed outwardly nothing that is not common to all, and quite ordinary. They fulfilled the duties of religion and of their state as others do and in apparently the same way. For the rest, if one scrutinizes their conduct, nothing can be discovered either striking or peculiar; all follows the same course of ordinary events. That which might single them out is not discernible; it is that dependence on the supreme will which arranges all things for them, and in which they habitually live. When God gives himself to a soul in this way, the ordinary sequence of life becomes extraordinary. This is why nothing extraordinary appears outwardly; because it is extraordinary in itself and consequently does not need the ornament of marvels which have nothing to do with it. (*AII.2.4.*)

Of course, this correspondence should not surprise us, for here (in Caussade's own words) is 'the spirituality of all the ages'— the hidden way of love which is nothing less than the royal road to paradise.

## Père de Caussade's prayer for obtaining
## holy self-abandonment

O my God, when will it please you to give me the grace of remaining habitually in that union of my will with your adorable will, in which, without our saying anything, all is said, and in which we do everything by letting you act. In this perfect union of wills we perform immense tasks because we work more in conformity with your good pleasure; and yet we are dispensed from all toil because we place the care of everything in your hands, and think of nothing but of reposing completely in you—a delightful state which even in the absence of all feelings of faith gives the soul an interior and altogether spiritual relish. Let me say then unceasingly through the habitual disposition of my heart: "*Fiat!* Yes, my God, yes, everything that you please. May your holy desires be fulfilled in everything. I give up my own which are blind, perverse and corrupted by that miserable self-love which is the mortal enemy of your grace and your love, of your glory and my own sanctification."

## A prayer in time of temptation

O God, keep me by your grace from all sin; but as for the pain which makes my self-love suffer, and for the holy humiliations which crucify my pride, I accept them with all my heart not so much as the effects of your justice but rather as the blessings of your great mercy. Have pity on me then, dear Lord, and help me.

From *Self-Abandonment to Divine Providence,* trans. Algar Thorold (Burns & Oates, 1959) p.449.

# BIBLIOGRAPHY

Quotations from the works of Jean-Pierre de Caussade are from the following English translations:

*On Prayer. Spiritual Instructions on the Various States of Prayer according to the doctrine of Bossuet, Bishop of Meux*, translated by Algar Thorold with an introduction by John Chapman (Burns & Oates, 1931; revised edition, 1949). Here referred to as *OP*.

*Abandonment to Divine Providence*, translated by E.J. Strickland from the standard French edition of P.H.Ramière (The Catholic Records Press, Exeter 1921). As well as the treatise on abandonment, this edition also contains the seven 'books' of letters and counsels.

Quotations from the *Treatise on Self-Abandonment* are here referred to as *A* and those from the *Letters* as *L*. For example, *A*II.1.7 means Book 2, Chapter 1, Section 7 of the *Treatise*; *L*V.14 means Letter 14 of Caussade's fifth 'book'.

References are also applicable to the translation by Algar Thorold, *Self-Abandonment to Divine Providence*, ed. John Joyce SJ, with an introduction by David Knowles (Burns & Oates, 1959).

## Notes

1   From 'A Biographical Sketch' in *Self-Abandonment to Divine Providence* (tr. Thorold, 1959) p.xxi.
2   Aelred Squire, *Asking the Fathers* (SPCK 1973; pbk edn. 1994) p.216.
3   Simon Tugwell, *Ways of Imperfection* (Darton, Longman & Todd, 1984) p.208.

[4] *Instructions spirituelles, en forme de dialogue sur les divers états d'oraisons, suivants la doctrine de Bossuet,* (English translation *On Prayer* by Algar Thorold, 1931).

[5] *OP* p.10.

[6] Thomas Merton, *Contemplative Prayer* (Darton, Longman & Todd, 1973) p.21.

[7] Richard MacKenna, *Is Anyone There?* (Collins: Fount Paperbacks, 1987) p.107

[8] Thomas Merton, *Contemplative Prayer,* p.85.

[9] *The Ladder of Perfection,* trans. Leo Sherley-Price (Penguin Books, 1957) II.25, p.169.

[10] St John of the Cross, quoted by Ruth Burrows, *Ascent to Love: The Spiritual Teaching of St John of the Cross,* (Darton, Longman & Todd, 1987) p.6

[11] *The Little Way: The Spirituality of Thérèse of Lisieux,* (English translation 1979) p.13.

[12] *Poèsies* 54 line 17; quoted Simon Tugwell OP, *Ways of Imperfection* (Darton, Longman & Todd, 1984) p.219.

## ALSO PUBLISHED BY SLG PRESS

THE SIMPLICITY OF PRAYER
by Mother Mary Clare SLG                                    £0.75

PRAYER OF THE HEART by Sandy Ryrie          £1.50

GEORGE HERBERT, PRIEST AND POET
by Kenneth Mason                                            £2.00

EVELYN UNDERHILL, ANGLICAN MYSTIC
by A.M Ramsey and A.M. Allchin                       £2.50

ST THÉRÈSE OF LISIEUX: Her Relevance for Today
by Sister Eileen Mary SLG                                 £1.50

THE DESERT OF THE HEART,Daily Readings with the
Desert Fathers by Benedicta Ward SLG            £1.75


A complete list of Fairacres Publications is available from
SLG Press,
Convent of the Incarnation, Fairacres, Oxford OX4 1TB